CONTENTS

Whatever the occasion, Mott's has a recipe for delighting your family and friends. *Mott's Classic Recipes* presents this treasured collection here in an easy-to-use format.

Whether you're planning a family barbecue or elegant dinner party, you'll find kitchen-tested ideas that are sure to please. Behind our diverse recipe assortment are the premium products that have made Mott's a trusted brand for over 150 years.

We hope you'll enjoy cooking with Mott's Classic Recipes. Bon Appetit!

Mott's family of fine foods includes:

Clamato—"The Deliciously Zesty Tomato Cocktail" is a Mott's original and a hit across the continent. Tasty by itself or mixed, Clamato adds flavor to the moment.

Grandma's Molasses—For over a century, quality-driven chefs have enhanced their cooking with Grandma's Molasses. Grandma's adds to, but never overpowers, the distinctive flavor of recipes. Made from the juice of sun-ripened sugar cane, Grandma's is the "surprise" all-natural sweetener.

Hawaiian Punch—Since 1934, customers have been drawn to Hawaiian Punch in ever-growing numbers. That fruit juicy taste packs a punch in five delicious flavors: Fruit Juicy Red, Grape Geyser, Orange Ocean, Strawberry Surfin' and Tropical Fruit.

Holland House Cooking Wines—These fine, full-strength wines keep longer than table wine, do not require refrigeration and will enhance the flavor of virtually any dish. Available in six flavors: White, White with Lemon, Red, Sherry, Marsala and Vermouth.

Holland House Mixers—For more than 100 years, Holland House has brought great taste to American homes. Holland House invented the liquid cocktail mix and now boasts a full line of products to satisfy every taste.

Mauna La'i—Taste the unique, authentic Hawaiian flavors of Mauna La'i. Available in four delicious tropical flavors: Island Guava, Paradise Passion, ¡Mango Mango! and Mandarin Papaya. Mauna La'i—Taste Paradise.

Mott's Apple Juice—An icon for more than 150 years, Mott's is America's #1 brand of apple juice. A refreshing drink by itself, Mott's apple juice makes marinades, punches and other foods even more delicious.

Mott's Apple Sauce—America's #1 brand of apple sauce, Mott's offers five delicious flavors (original, natural, chunky, cinnamon and homestyle.) Wonderful as a side dish or snack, Mott's apple sauce is also a marvelous ingredient for a wide variety of dishes. Diet-conscious cooks who substitute Mott's apple sauce for oil will appreciate how it produces appetizing treats with lower fat content.

Mr & Mrs T Mixers—From America's favorite Bloody Mary to the perfect Piña Colada, Mr & Mrs T has the mix for everyone's favorite drinks.

THE BEST BRUNCHES

GRANDMA'S Bran Muffins

2½ cups bran flakes, divided
1 cup raisins
1 cup boiling water
½ cup canola oil
1 cup GRANDMA'S Molasses
2 eggs, beaten
2 cups buttermilk
2¾ cups all-purpose flour
2½ teaspoons baking soda
½ teaspoon salt

Heat oven to 400°F. In medium bowl, mix 1 cup bran flakes, raisins and water. Set aside. In large bowl, combine remaining ingredients. Mix in bran-raisin mixture. Pour into greased muffin pan cups. Fill ⅔ full and bake for 20 minutes. Remove muffins and place on rack to cool. *Makes 48 muffins*

Paradise Breakfast Syrup

1 cup MAUNA LA'I Paradise Passion Juice Drink
¾ cup sugar

Combine juice drink and sugar in medium saucepan. Bring to boil stirring frequently. Reduce heat and simmer 15 minutes, stirring occasionally. Remove from heat. Let cool to thicken. Store in refrigerator.   *Makes ¾ cup*

Apple Pan Dowdy

5 apples, peeled, cored and sliced
1 cup bread flour
2 teaspoons baking powder
¾ teaspoon salt, divided
2 tablespoons shortening
¼ cup sugar
¼ cup GRANDMA'S Molasses
½ teaspoon each cinnamon and nutmeg
¾ cup milk
½ cup hot water

Heat oven to 350°F. Grease 12X9-inch baking dish and layer apples onto bottom. In mixing bowl, sift in flour, baking powder and ¼ teaspoon salt. Stir slightly. Beat shortening into flour mixture. Add sugar, molasses, cinnamon, nutmeg and remaining ½ teaspoon salt. Pour in milk and water; mix until smooth. Pour mixture over apples. Bake for 35 to 40 minutes. Turn onto plate with apple side up. Serve with whipped cream, if desired.
Makes 8 servings

Peanut Berry Smoothie

4 ounces MR & MRS T Strawberry Daiquiri Mix
2 ounces yogurt (non-fat or regular)
2 tablespoons peanut butter
½ cup orange juice
½ cup ice
  Dash of nutmeg (for garnish)

Blend first 5 ingredients in a blender until smooth. Pour into glass and sprinkle with nutmeg.

Makes 2 (8-ounce) smoothies

Nut and Raisin Bread

2 cups all-purpose flour
1½ cups bread flour
½ cup corn meal
½ cup brown sugar
4 teaspoons baking powder
1 teaspoon salt
1 cup chopped raisins
¾ cup chopped nuts
2 cups milk
½ cup GRANDMA'S Molasses
¼ teaspoon baking soda

Heat oven to 375°F. In large bowl, sift and mix dry ingredients; add raisins and nuts. Add milk and mix well. In another bowl combine molasses and baking soda; add to flour mixture. Knead into a dough. Bake in oven until golden brown, about 45 minutes.

Makes 8 servings

Chesapeake Bay Bloody Mary

1 cup ice
4 ounces **MR & MRS T Bloody Mary Mix**
1½ ounces vodka
½ ounce **ROSE'S Lime Juice**
¼ teaspoon crab boil seasoning (or favorite seafood spice blend)
Lime wedge (for garnish)
Celery stick (for garnish)

Fill a tall glass with ice; add next 4 ingredients. Stir well and garnish with lime wedge or celery stick. *Makes 1 serving*

Cornflake Pudding

4 cups cornflakes
1 egg
4 cups milk
⅔ cup **GRANDMA'S Molasses**
1 teaspoon salt
1 teaspoon cinnamon

Heat oven to 300°F. Place corn flakes in 1½-quart soufflé dish. Beat egg; add milk, molasses, salt and cinnamon in large bowl. Pour over corn flakes. Mix well. Bake for 1½ hours.

Makes 4 servings

Chesapeake Bay Bloody Mary and Spanish Omelet (page 16)

Lemon Chicken Salad

½ cup **HOLLAND HOUSE** White with Lemon
    Cooking Wine
1 pound boneless, skinless chicken breasts
1 cup snow peas, blanched, roughly chopped
¾ cup sliced celery
¼ cup sliced scallions
½ cup mayonnaise
1 teaspoon grated lemon peel
    Black pepper, to taste
½ cup toasted slivered almonds
    Lettuce leaves, as needed

1. Place cooking wine and chicken in large saucepan. Add enough water to cover. Bring to a boil; reduce heat. Simmer 10 minutes or until chicken is tender and cooked through. Let chicken cool in liquid for 45 minutes. Drain; cut chicken into bite-sized pieces.

2. In large bowl, combine chicken, snow peas, celery, scallions, mayonnaise, lemon peel and pepper. Cover and refrigerate 1 to 2 hours to blend flavors. Just before serving, stir in almonds. To serve, spoon chicken salad onto lettuce-lined plates.

Makes 4 servings

Quick Apple Punch (page 12)
and Lemon Chicken Salad

GRANDMA'S Molasses
Banana Bread

1 cup whole wheat flour
¾ cup all-purpose flour
2 teaspoons baking soda
½ teaspoon salt
½ cup softened butter
1 egg
1 cup **GRANDMA'S Molasses**
3 large mashed bananas
½ cup chopped walnuts

Heat oven to 350°F. In medium bowl, combine flours, baking soda, and salt. Set aside. Cream butter in large bowl. Beat in egg, molasses, bananas and walnuts. Mix in dry ingredients just until blended. Pour mixture into greased and floured 9X5-loaf pan. Bake 50 to 60 minutes. Cool on wire rack.   *Makes 1 loaf*

Quick Apple Punch

4 cups **MOTT'S Apple Juice**
2 cups cranberry juice cocktail
2 tablespoons lemon juice
1 liter ginger ale, chilled
Crushed ice, as needed

In large bowl, combine apple juice, cranberry juice, and lemon juice. Fifteen minutes before serving, add ginger ale and crushed ice. Do not stir.   *Makes 15 servings*

Hot Cross Buns

1 package (14 ounces) active dry yeast
¼ cup warm water (105° to 115°F)
¾ cup warm milk
¼ cup **GRANDMA'S** Molasses
4 tablespoons (½-stick) butter, softened
2 eggs
1½ teaspoons salt
3½ cups all-purpose flour, divided
1 teaspoon cinnamon
½ teaspoon nutmeg
¼ teaspoon allspice
½ cup currants or raisins
2 tablespoons chopped candied citron

1. In large bowl, stir yeast into water and let stand several minutes to dissolve. Combine milk, molasses, butter, eggs and salt in large bowl; beat well. Add yeast mixture; mix well. Beat in 1½ cups flour, cinnamon, nutmeg and allspice. Cover bowl and let rise about 1 hour or until bubbly or double in bulk.

2. Add remaining 2 cups flour and blend well, adding additional flour if necessary to make dough firm enough to handle. Turn onto floured surface; knead dough until firm and elastic. Add currants and citron during last 5 minutes of kneading. Place dough in greased bowl; cover and let rise until double in bulk.

3. Heat oven to 375°F. Punch dough down; turn onto lightly floured surface. Roll into 14X10-inch rectangle, about ½-inch thick. Cut dough with 2½- to 3-inch round cutter; place buns about 1-inch apart on greased baking sheets. Gather up scraps, reroll and continue cutting until all dough has been used. Let rise, uncovered, until double in bulk.

4. Just before baking, use floured scissors to snip cross in tip of each bun, cutting about ½-inch deep. Bake about 15 minutes or until tops of buns are golden brown. Remove from oven and transfer to rack to cool.   *Makes 12 buns*

Spicy Southwest Quiche

2 (9-inch) prepared pie shells
6 eggs
1 cup heavy cream
1 cup **CLAMATO** Tomato Cocktail
½ teaspoon salt
⅛ teaspoon white pepper
⅛ teaspoon nutmeg
1 package (10 ounces) frozen chopped spinach,
    thawed and well drained
1 small onion, chopped
6 black olives, sliced
1 medium red pepper, chopped
½ cup grated Swiss cheese

1. Heat oven to 425°F. Bake pie shells for 15 minutes; remove and set aside. *Reduce oven temperature to 350°F.*

2. In large bowl, beat eggs, cream, Clamato, salt, white pepper and nutmeg. Stir in spinach and onion. Divide custard mixture between baked pie shells. Arrange olives and red pepper on top of custard. Sprinkle with cheese.

3. Bake for 30 to 40 minutes or until centers are set.

Makes 2 quiches or 12 servings

*Spicy Buffalo Mary (page 16)
and Spicy Southwest Quiche*

Spicy Buffalo Mary

  1 cup ice
  4 ounces MR & MRS T Bloody Mary Rich and
      Spicy Mix
1 ½ ounces vodka
  ½ ounce ROSE'S Lime Juice
  ½ teaspoon hot sauce
  1 teaspoon blue cheese, crumbled
      Celery stick

Fill a tall glass with ice; add next 4 ingredients. Stir well. Press
blue cheese crumbles into celery stick. Place blue cheese-stuffed
celery stick into glass.   *Makes 1 serving*

Spanish Omelet

  4 eggs
  3 tablespoons CLAMATO Tomato Cocktail
  1 teaspoon salt
  1 teaspoon pepper
  1 teaspoon olive oil
  1 medium onion, minced
  3 mushrooms, sliced
  1 tablespoon finely chopped jalapeño
  2 slices of ham
  1 slice American cheese

In medium bowl, whisk together eggs, Clamato, salt and pepper.
In medium non-stick skillet, heat olive oil over medium-high
heat. Add onions and mushrooms and sauté until lightly
browned. Remove and set aside. Add egg mixture to skillet.
Cook until eggs set slightly, about 2 minutes. Add jalapeño, ham,
American cheese and reserved onions and mushrooms to
center of omelet. When eggs are almost fully cooked and cheese
has melted fold omelet in half. Tilt pan away from you and push
omelet toward the far end of skillet. Turn omelet onto plate.
                                              Makes 1 omelet

Gingerbread with Fresh Fruit Sauce

GINGERBREAD:
   2 cups all-purpose flour
   1/4 cup sugar
   1 teaspoon baking soda
   1 teaspoon ginger
   1/2 teaspoon cinnamon
   1/4 teaspoon salt
   1 cup GRANDMA'S Molasses
   1/2 cup butter, softened
   2 eggs
   1/2 cup milk

FRESH FRUIT SAUCE:
   1/4 cup GRANDMA'S Molasses
   1/4 cup firmly packed brown sugar
   1 tablespoon cornstarch
   1 cup orange juice
   2 tablespoons butter
   1 teaspoon grated orange peel
   1 teaspoon cinnamon
   1 can (11 ounces) orange segments, drained
   1 can (8 ounces) pineapple chunks, drained
   1 cup green grapes, halved

1. Heat oven to 350°F. Grease 9-inch springform pan. In medium bowl, combine first six ingredients; set aside. In large bowl, combine molasses, butter, eggs and milk; mix well. Combine flour mixture with molasses mixture. Pour into prepared pan. Bake 35 minutes or until toothpick inserted in center comes out clean. Cool 15 minutes. Remove side of pan; cool on wire rack.

2. In medium saucepan, combine molasses, brown sugar and cornstarch; mix well. Stir in orange juice. Bring to boil. Cook over medium heat for 5 minutes or until thickened, stirring constantly. Remove from heat. Add butter, orange peel and cinnamon; mix well. Stir in remaining ingredients.

Makes 9 servings

Warm Ginger Almond Chicken Salad

DRESSING:
- $1/3$ cup **GRANDMA'S Molasses**
- $1/4$ cup oil
- $1/4$ cup cider vinegar
- 1 teaspoon finely chopped ginger root or $1/2$ teaspoon ground ginger
- 1 teaspoon soy sauce
- $1/2$ teaspoon salt
- Dash hot pepper sauce

SALAD:
- 1 pound boneless, skinless chicken breasts, cut into thin strips
- 4 cups, torn mixed greens
- 1 cup (2 medium) shredded carrots
- $1/4$ cup chopped green onions
- 1 tablespoon cornstarch
- 2 tablespoons water
- $1/4$ cup sliced almonds, toasted

1. In medium bowl, combine all dressing ingredients. Add chicken strips; blend well. Cover; refrigerate 1 to 2 hours. In serving bowl, combine greens, carrots and green onions. Refrigerate.

2. In large skillet, combine chicken and dressing. Bring to a boil, cooking and stirring until chicken is no longer pink, about 3 to 5 minutes. In small bowl, combine cornstarch and water; blend well. Stir into chicken mixture. Cook until mixture thickens, stirring constantly. Spoon hot chicken mixture over vegetables; toss to combine. Sprinkle with almonds. Serve immediately.

Makes 4 servings

Warm Ginger Almond Chicken Salad

CLASSIC CELEBRATIONS

Orange Pecan Pie

3 eggs
½ cup **GRANDMA'S** Molasses
½ cup light corn syrup
¼ cup orange juice
1 teaspoon grated orange peel
1 teaspoon vanilla
1½ cups whole pecan halves
1 (9-inch) unbaked pie shell
Whipping cream (optional)

Heat oven to 350°F. In large bowl, beat eggs. Add molasses, corn syrup, orange juice, orange peel, and vanilla; beat until well blended. Stir in pecans. Pour into unbaked pie shell. Bake 30 to 45 minutes or until filling sets. Cool on wire rack. Serve with whipping cream, if desired.   *Makes 8 servings*

Hot Spiced Toddy

1 cup **MAUNA LA'I ¡Mango Mango! Juice Drink**
   Dash ground cinnamon
⅛ **cup dark rum (optional)**
1 **tablespoon brown sugar**
2 **teaspoons butter (optional)**
1 **cinnamon stick**

Heat Mauna La'i ¡Mango Mango! Juice Drink and cinnamon in a small saucepan. Add rum, if desired, brown sugar, butter, if desired, in a mug. Pour hot juice drink into mug and stir gently. Garnish with cinnamon stick.

Makes 1 serving

Lemon-Herb Roast Chicken

⅓ **cup lemon juice**
¼ **cup HOLLAND HOUSE Vermouth Cooking Wine**
¼ **cup oil**
½ **teaspoon dried rosemary leaves**
½ **teaspoon dried thyme leaves**
1 **garlic clove, minced**
1 **whole chicken (2½ to 3) pounds**

1. In large plastic bowl, combine lemon juice, cooking wine, oil, rosemary, thyme and garlic; mix well. Add chicken, turning to coat all sides. Cover; refrigerate 1 to 2 hours, turning several times.

2. Heat oven to 375°F. Remove chicken from marinade; reserving marinade. Twist wing tips under back. Place chicken, breast side up, on rack in shallow pan. Brush with marinade. Roast 55 to 65 minutes, or until chicken is tender and juices run clear, brushing with marinade* halfway through roasting. Remove chicken to cutting board; let stand 5 to 10 minutes before carving.

Makes 4 servings

*Do not baste during last 5 minutes of cooking.

Bananas with Caramel Sauce

3 or 4 bananas, peeled
2 tablespoons orange or lemon juice
2 tablespoons butter
¼ cup whipping cream
¼ cup **GRANDMA'S** Molasses
¼ teaspoon cinnamon
¼ teaspoon nutmeg
¼ cup walnut halves

1. Slice bananas in half lengthwise, then crosswise. Place bananas in large bowl; brush with orange juice. Set aside. Place butter in 9-inch microwave-safe pie plate.

2. Microwave at HIGH power for 30 seconds or until melted. Stir in cream, molasses, cinnamon and nutmeg. Microwave at HIGH for 1½ to 2 minutes or until thickened, stirring once. Add bananas and walnuts; mix well to coat. Microwave at HIGH for 30 seconds or until bananas are tender. Serve immediately over waffles, ice cream or orange slices.   *Makes 4 servings*

Roast Beef with Red Wine Gravy

2 tablespoons oil
  Salt and black pepper
1 sirloin tip roast (3 to 4 pounds)
2 tablespoons all-purpose flour
1 jar (7 ounces) cocktail onions, drained
1 can (14½ ounces) beef broth
2 tablespoons **HOLLAND HOUSE** Red Cooking
  Wine

Heat oven to 350°F. Heat oil in Dutch oven. Season roast to taste with salt and pepper; brown on all sides. Remove from Dutch oven. Drain excess fat, reserving ¼ cup drippings in Dutch oven. Sprinkle flour over reserved drippings. Cook over medium heat until lightly browned, stirring constantly. Add roast and onions to Dutch oven. Cook for 1¾ to 2¼ hours or until desired doneness. Remove roast onto cutting board. Let stand 5 to 10 minutes before slicing. Gradually stir in beef broth and cooking wine. Bring to a boil; reduce heat. Cook until gravy thickens. Slice roast and arrange with onions on serving platter. Serve with gravy.   *Makes 6 servings*

Roast Beef with Red Wine Gravy
and Sherried Mushrooms
(page 26)

Sherried Mushrooms

½ cup butter
1 cup **HOLLAND HOUSE** Sherry Cooking Wine
1 garlic clove, crushed
18 fresh mushrooms, sliced
Salt and black pepper

Melt butter in medium skillet over medium heat. Add cooking wine and garlic. Add mushrooms; cook until tender, about 5 minutes, stirring frequently. Season to taste with salt and pepper. *Makes 2 to 3 servings*

Easy Cheese Fondue

1 pound low-sodium Swiss cheese (Gruyère, Emmentaler or combination of both), divided
2 tablespoons cornstarch
1 garlic clove, crushed
1 cup **HOLLAND HOUSE** White or White with Lemon Cooking Wine
1 tablespoon kirsch or cherry brandy (optional)
Pinch nutmeg
Ground black pepper

1. In medium bowl, coat cheese with cornstarch; set aside. Rub inside of ceramic fondue pot or heavy saucepan with garlic; discard garlic. Bring wine to gentle simmer over medium heat. Gradually stir in cheese to ensure smooth fondue. Once smooth, stir in brandy, if desired. Garnish with nutmeg and pepper.

2. Serve with bite-sized chunks of French bread, broccoli, cauliflower, tart apples or pears. Spear with fondue forks or wooden skewers. *Makes 1¼ cups*

Easy Cheese Fondue

Easy Oven Beef Stew

2 pounds boneless beef stew meat, cut into 1½ inch
   cubes
1 can (16 ounces) tomatoes, undrained, cut up
1 can (10½ ounces) condensed beef broth
1 cup **HOLLAND HOUSE** Red Cooking Wine
1 tablespoon Italian seasonings spice*
6 potatoes, peeled, quartered
6 carrots cut into 2-inch pieces
3 celery stalks cut into 1-inch pieces
2 medium onions, peeled, quartered
⅓ cup instant tapioca
¼ teaspoon black pepper
   Chopped fresh parsley

*You can substitute 1½ teaspoons each of basil and oregano for Italian
seasonings.*

Heat oven to 325°F. Combine all ingredients except parsley in
Dutch oven; cover. Bake 2½ to 3 hours or until meat and
vegetables are tender. Garnish with parsley.

Makes 8 servings

English Bread Pudding

  2 cups hot milk
½ small loaf of bread, sliced
  1 tablespoon butter
  1 egg
½ cup GRANDMA'S Molasses
½ cup sugar
  1 teaspoon cinnamon
½ teaspoon nutmeg
  1 cup chopped raisins
½ cup chopped nuts

Heat oven to 350°F. In large bowl, pour milk over bread and butter. In another bowl, combine egg, molasses, sugar, cinnamon and nutmeg. When bread is cool pour egg mixture, raisins and nuts over it. Bake 2 hours or until mixture is set and tip of a knife comes out clean. Serve with whipped cream.

Makes 4 servings

Golden Harvest Punch

  4 cups MOTT'S Apple Juice
  4 cups orange juice
  3 liters club soda
  1 quart orange sherbet
  5 pound bag ice cubes (optional)

Combine apple juice, orange juice and club soda in punch bowl. Add scoops of sherbet or ice.   *Makes 25 servings*

Peach Blueberry Cheesecake

CRUST:
- 1 ½ cups crushed graham cracker crumbs
- ½ cup crushed gingersnap cookies
- 5 tablespoons butter, melted

FILLING:
- 2 packages (8 ounces each) cream cheese, softened
- ¾ cup sugar
- ½ cup **GRANDMA'S** Molasses
- 7 egg yolks
- 2 tablespoons lemon juice
- 1 ½ teaspoons vanilla extract
- ½ teaspoon salt
- 3 cups sour cream

TOPPING:
- 1 can (16 ounces) peach slices, drained
  Fresh blueberries
- 2 tablespoons peach or apricot preserves, melted

1. Heat oven to 350°F. Grease 9-inch springform pan. In small bowl, combine crust ingredients; press over bottom and half way up side of pan. Refrigerate. Place large roasting pan filled with 1 inch hot water on middle rack of oven. In large bowl, beat cream cheese and sugar until very smooth, about 3 minutes. Beat in molasses. Add egg yolks, beating until batter is smooth. Add lemon juice, vanilla and salt; beat until well incorporated. Beat in sour cream just until blended. Pour batter into prepared crust.

2. Place cheesecake in large roasting pan. Bake 45 minutes. Turn oven off without opening door and let cake cool 1 hour. Transfer cheesecake to wire rack (center will be jiggly) and cool to room temperature, about 1 hour. Cover pan with plastic wrap and refrigerate overnight. Remove side of pan. Top with peach slices and blueberries. Brush fruit with preserves.

Makes 12 to 16 servings

Peach Blueberry Cheesecake

Shrimp Creole Pronto

2 tablespoons oil
1 cup chopped onions
1 cup chopped celery
1 green bell pepper, chopped
2 garlic cloves, minced
2 cups chopped, peeled tomatoes
1 can (8 ounces) tomato sauce
½ cup **HOLLAND HOUSE Marsala Cooking Wine**
¼ teaspoon freshly ground black pepper
1 pound fresh or frozen, thawed, uncooked shrimp, peeled, deveined
¼ to ½ teaspoon hot pepper sauce
4 cups hot cooked rice or 1 (10-ounce) package of egg noodles, cooked, drained

Heat oil in large saucepan over medium-high heat. Add onions, celery, bell pepper and garlic; cook 2 to 3 minutes. Add tomatoes; cook 2 to 3 minutes, stirring occasionally. Add remaining ingredients except rice; cook 2 to 3 minutes or until shrimp turn pink. Serve over hot cooked rice.

Makes 4 servings

Shrimp Creole Pronto

Boston Brown Bread

2½ cups rye flour
1 cup corn meal
1 teaspoon salt
1 teaspoon baking soda
2 cups hot water
1 cup GRANDMA'S Molasses
1 cup raisins (optional)

Heat oven to 375°F. In large bowl, mix dry ingredients. In medium bowl, combine water and molasses; pour into dry ingredients. Stir until smooth. Add raisins, if desired. Pour into greased molds, two-thirds full. Bake until golden brown, about 40 minutes.   *Makes 8 servings*

Plantation Gingerbread

2 cups all-purpose flour
2 teaspoon cinnamon
1½ teaspoons ginger
1 teaspoon baking powder
½ teaspoon baking soda
½ teaspoon salt
⅓ cup melted shortening
1 cup GRANDMA'S Molasses
½ cup buttermilk
1 egg
½ cup MOTT'S Apple Sauce
½ cup raisins

Heat oven to 350°F. In large bowl, combine dry ingredients. In another large bowl, combine shortening and molasses until well blended. Add molasses mixture, buttermilk and egg to flour mixture. Stir in apple sauce and raisins. Bake in greased 9-inch square pan for about 35 minutes or until toothpick inserted in center comes out clean.   *Makes 4 servings*

Classic Apple Sauce Cheesecake

2½ cups bran flakes, divided
¾ cup butter
¼ cup firmly packed light brown sugar
2 packages (8 ounces each) cream cheese, softened
¾ cup sugar
3 eggs
2 cups MOTT'S Apple Sauce, divided
1 teaspoon vanilla extract

1. Heat oven to 350°F. Finely roll 2 cups bran flakes. Place crumbs in large bowl; stir in butter and brown sugar. Press mixture firmly on bottom and up side of 9-inch pie plate; set aside. In bowl, beat cream cheese, sugar and eggs until smooth.

2. Stir in 1 cup apple sauce and vanilla; pour into bran crust. Bake 40 to 45 minutes until center is just set. Gently spread remaining 1 cup apple sauce over cheesecake; cool. Chill at least 4 hours. Sprinkle with remaining ½ cup bran before serving.

Makes 10 servings

Baked Apples

2 tablespoons sugar
2 tablespoons GRANDMA'S Molasses
2 tablespoons raisins, chopped
2 tablespoons walnuts, chopped
6 apples, cored

Heat oven to 350°F. In medium bowl, combine sugar, molasses, raisins and walnuts. Fill apple cavities with molasses mixture. Place in 13X9-inch baking dish. Pour ½ cup hot water over the apples and bake 25 minutes or until soft.   *Makes 6 servings*

Marinated Pork Roast

½ cup GRANDMA'S Molasses
½ cup Dijon mustard
¼ cup tarragon vinegar
  Boneless pork loin roast (3 to 4 pounds)

1. In large plastic bowl, combine molasses, mustard and tarragon vinegar; mix well. Add pork to molasses mixture, turning to coat all sides. Marinate 1 to 2 hours at room temperature or overnight covered in refrigerator, turning several times.

2. Heat oven to 325°F. Remove pork from marinade; reserve marinade. Place pork in shallow roasting pan. Cook for 1 to 2 hours or until meat thermometer inserted into thickest part of roast reaches 160°F, basting with marinade* every 30 minutes; discard remaining marinade.   *Makes 6 to 8 servings*

Do not baste during last 5 minutes of cooking.

Top to Bottom: Baked Apple and
Marinated Pork Roast

Manhattan Clam Chowder

2 pieces bacon, diced
1 large red bell pepper, diced
1 large green bell pepper, diced
1 celery stalk, chopped
1 carrot, peeled and chopped
1 small onion, chopped
1 clove garlic, finely chopped
2 cups bottled clam juice
1 cup CLAMATO Tomato Cocktail
2 medium potatoes, peeled and diced
1 large tomato, chopped
1 teaspoon oregano
½ teaspoon black pepper
2 cups fresh or canned clams, chopped (about 24 shucked clams)

In heavy 4-quart saucepan, sauté bacon, peppers, celery, carrot, onion and garlic over medium heat until tender, about 10 minutes. (Do not brown bacon.) Add clam juice, Clamato, potatoes, tomato, oregano and pepper. Simmer 35 minutes or until potatoes are tender. Add clams; cook 5 minutes more.

Makes 8 servings

Manhattan Clam Chowder

ETHNIC ENTERTAINING

Fajitas

½ cup chopped onion
¼ cup **GRANDMA'S** Molasses
¼ cup oil
 2 tablespoons **ROSE'S** lime juice
 2 tablespoons chili powder
½ teaspoon oregano leaves
 2 garlic cloves, minced
 1 pound boneless top round or sirloin steak, cut into
   thin strips
10 flour tortillas (8 to 10 inches), softened
½ cup (4 ounces) shredded Monterey Jack cheese
 2 cups refried beans
 2 tomatoes, chopped
1½ cups shredded lettuce
 1 avocado, chopped
 1 cup salsa
   Sour cream

1. In medium plastic bowl, combine onions, molasses, oil, lime juice, chili powder, oregano and garlic. Mix well. Add steak, stir to coat. Cover; marinate 4 to 6 hours or overnight, stirring occasionally.

2. In large skillet, stir-fry meat mixture 5 minutes or until brown. To serve, place meat in center of each tortilla; top with cheese, refried beans, tomatoes, lettuce, avocado and salsa. Fold up tortilla. Serve with sour cream. *Makes 5 servings*

Basil Shrimp Fettuccine

3 tablespoons butter
3 tablespoons olive oil
2 tomatoes, peeled, seeded and chopped
1 garlic clove, minced
1/3 cup evaporated skim milk
1/2 cup **HOLLAND HOUSE** White Cooking Wine
1/2 cup fresh basil, chopped
1/2 cup shrimp, peeled and deveined
4 tablespoons Parmesan cheese, grated and divided
4 tablespoons fresh parsley, chopped and divided
1 pound fettuccine, cooked and drained

Melt butter and oil in medium saucepan over medium heat. Add tomatoes and garlic; simmer until tomatoes are softened. Add milk and cooking wine; simmer 10 minutes. Stir in basil and shrimp; simmer 3 minutes or until shrimp turn pink and are opaque. Add 2 tablespoons cheese and 2 tablespoons parsley. Serve over cooked fettuccine. Sprinkle with remaining 2 tablespoons each, cheese and parsley.

Makes 4 to 6 servings

Mexican Fiesta Soup

3 cans (14½ ounces each) chicken broth
2 cups cooked chicken, cubed
1 cup peeled potatoes, cubed
1 cup chopped carrots
1 cup chopped onions
1 cup chopped celery
1 can (17 ounces) whole kernel corn, undrained
1 can (12 ounces) vegetable or tomato juice
1 cup tomato salsa
½ cup **HOLLAND HOUSE** Vermouth Cooking Wine
1 can (4 ounces) chopped green chilies, undrained
¼ cup chopped fresh cilantro (optional)
   Shredded Monterey Jack cheese (optional)
   Tortilla chips (optional)

In large saucepan, combine chicken broth, chicken, potatoes, carrots, onions, celery, corn, vegetable juice, salsa, cooking wine, green chilies and cilantro, if desired, and place over medium-high heat. Bring to a boil; reduce heat. Simmer 20 to 30 minutes or until vegetables are tender. Serve with cheese and tortilla chips as garnishes, if desired.   *Makes 8 (1½-cup) servings*

Chicken Marsala

1 tablespoon butter
2 boneless skinless chicken breasts, halved
1 cup sliced carrots
1 cup sliced fresh mushrooms
1/3 cup chicken broth
1/3 cup **HOLLAND HOUSE** Marsala Cooking Wine

Melt butter in skillet over medium-high heat. Add chicken; cook 5 minutes. Turn chicken over, add remaining ingredients. Bring to a boil; simmer 15 to 20 minutes until juices run clear. Serve over cooked fettuccine, if desired. *Makes 4 servings*

Gazpacho

1 small onion*, diced
2 large red bell peppers, seeded and diced
1 medium cucumber, peeled and diced
2 large ripe tomatoes, cored
1/4 cup olive oil
2 tablespoons red wine vinegar
1 clove garlic, minced
1/2 teaspoon salt
1/4 teaspoon cumin
1/2 teaspoon dried thyme leaves
1/4 teaspoon black pepper
4 cups **CLAMATO** Tomato Cocktail
*Reserve portion of onion, pepper and cucumber for garnish.

Place onion, bell pepper and cucumber in food processor or blender. Add tomatoes, oil, vinegar garlic, salt, cumin, thyme and pepper; process until smooth. Stir in Clamato. Adjust seasonings as needed. Refrigerate until well chilled. Garnish with reserved onion, pepper and cucumber. *Makes 8 servings*

Chicken Marsala

Sensational Spaghetti and Meatballs

SAUCE
- 2 tablespoons butter
- ½ cup chopped onion
- 1 cup chicken broth
- ½ cup HOLLAND HOUSE White Cooking Wine
- 1 can (28 ounces) plum tomatoes, puréed and strained
- 1 can (6 ounces) tomato paste
- 3 tablespoons chopped fresh basil or 3 teaspoons dried basil leaves
- ½ teaspoon sugar
- 1 cup whipping cream

MEATBALLS
- ¾ pound bulk Italian sausage
- ¾ pound ground beef
- ¼ cup dry breadcrumbs
- ¼ cup grated Parmesan cheese
- ¼ cup HOLLAND HOUSE Red Cooking Wine
- 1 egg, beaten
- 1 pound spaghetti, cooked and drained

1. Melt butter in medium saucepan. Add onion; cook until tender. Add chicken broth and cooking wine. Bring to a boil; boil until liquid is reduced to about ¾ cup. Add puréed tomatoes, tomato paste, basil and sugar. Bring to a boil; reduce heat. Simmer 30 to 45 minutes or until thickened, stirring occasionally. Gradually stir in whipping cream.

2. While sauce is cooking, prepare meatballs. Heat oven to 350°F. In medium bowl, combine all meatball ingredients; shape into ¾-inch balls. Place meatballs in 15½×10½×1-inch baking pan. Bake 20 minutes or until brown. Top cooked spaghetti with meatballs and sauce. *Makes 8 servings*

Chicken Wings Teriyaki

½ cup teriyaki sauce
¼ cup **HOLLAND HOUSE** Sherry Cooking Wine
2 tablespoons oil
2 tablespoons honey
1 teaspoon finely chopped peeled ginger
½ teaspoon five spice powder
¼ teaspoon sesame oil
2 cloves garlic, finely chopped
2 pounds chicken wings
¼ cup sliced scallions
1 tablespoon toasted sesame seeds

Heat oven to 375°F. In small bowl, combine teriyaki sauce, cooking wine, oil, honey, ginger, five spice powder, sesame oil and garlic. Pour into 13×9-inch pan. Add chicken wings, turning to coat all sides. Bake for 35 to 45 minutes or until chicken is tender and cooked through, turning once and basting occasionally with sauce.* Sprinkle with scallions and sesame seeds. *Makes 24 appetizers*

*Do not baste during last 5 minutes of grilling.

Swedish Apple Nut Strip

1½ cups all-purpose flour
3 tablespoons sugar, divided
½ teaspoon salt
½ cup butter
1 egg, slightly beaten
1 cup MOTT'S Cinnamon Apple Sauce
¼ cup finely chopped walnuts
1 teaspoon ground cinnamon

1. Heat oven to 375°F. In bowl, mix flour, 2 tablespoons sugar and salt; cut in butter until mixture is crumbly. Stir in egg; form dough into a ball. Cover; chill for 15 minutes. Divide dough in half. On lightly greased baking sheet, shape each half into a 10×2-inch rectangle. Make a 1-inch wide indentation down the center length of each rectangle; fill each with ½ cup of apple sauce.

2. Mix remaining 1 tablespoon sugar, walnuts and cinnamon; sprinkle on dough along sides of apple sauce filling. Bake 20 minutes. Cool slightly on wire rack. Cut into 1-inch diagonal slices. Cool completely. Store in airtight container.

Makes 20 bars

Belgian Wassail (page 50) and
Swedish Apple Nut Strip

Belgian Wassail

2 oranges
2 lemons
4 cups water
1 tablespoon allspice
2 cinnamon sticks
1 cup sugar
1 gallon MOTT'S Apple Juice

In large bowl, squeeze juice from oranges and lemons. Reserve the juice and rinds. In large saucepan boil water, orange and lemon rinds, allspice and cinnamon. Simmer 1 hour. Remove rinds and add sugar, apple juice and reserved juice. Stir to dissolve sugar. Serve hot. *Makes 20 servings*

Sweet 'n Sour Grape Fizz

3 ounces MR & MRS T Sweet & Sour Mix
3 ounces white grape juice
1½ ounces rum
½ ounce ROSE'S Lime Juice
1 ounce club soda
½ cup ice
Frozen grapes*

For frozen grapes, simply rinse grapes under cold running water and place in the freezer until frozen (15 to 20 minutes).

Pour first 5 ingredients into shaker with ice. Strain contents into glass and garnish with frozen grapes. *Makes 1 serving*

Broccoli Beef Stir-Fry

½ cup beef broth
4 tablespoons HOLLAND HOUSE Sherry Cooking
   Wine, divided
2 tablespoons soy sauce
1 tablespoon cornstarch
1 teaspoon sugar
2 tablespoons vegetable oil, divided
2 cups fresh broccoli florets
1 cup fresh snow peas
1 red bell pepper, cut into strips
1 pound boneless top round or sirloin steak, slightly
   frozen, cut into thin strips
1 clove garlic, minced
4 cups hot cooked rice

1. To make sauce, in small bowl, combine broth, 2 tablespoons of cooking wine, soy sauce, cornstarch and sugar. Mix well and set aside. In large skillet or wok, heat 1 tablespoon oil. Stir-fry broccoli, snow peas and bell pepper 1 minute. Add remaining 2 tablespoons cooking wine.

2. Cover; cook 1 to 2 minutes. Remove from pan. Heat remaining 1 tablespoon oil; add meat and garlic. Stir-fry 5 minutes or until meat is browned. Add sauce to meat; cook 2 to 3 minutes or until thickened, stirring frequently. Add vegetables and heat through. Serve over cooked rice.

Makes 4 servings

Piquant Veracruz Clams

    6 clams, opened*
    2 ounces bacon bits
    1 tablespoon **ROSE'S Lime Juice**
    3 ounces butter, slightly soft
    ¼ cup seasoned breadcrumbs
       Salt and black pepper

Ask your seafood supplier to provide you with the clam meat and their shells separately.

1. Preheat oven to 350°F. In a bowl, mix clam meat, bacon bits, lime juice, butter and breadcrumbs. Season to taste with salt and pepper.

2. Fill each clamshell with mixture and place on baking sheet in oven for 6 to 8 minutes, or until filling turns golden brown.

Makes 2 servings (3 clams each)

Sour Apple Margarita

    3 ounces MR & MRS T Margarita Mix
    1 ounce sour apple liqueur
  1 ½ ounces tequila
    ½ ounce **ROSE'S Lime Juice**
    ½ ounce **ROSE'S Triple Sec**
    ½ cup ice
    1 lime, sliced
       50/50 cinnamon/sugar mixture (optional)

Mix first 6 ingredients in shaker. Shake well. Coat rim of martini glass with lime and dip in cinnamon/sugar mixture, if desired. Strain into glass and serve.   *Makes 1 serving*

Sour Apple Margarita and
Piquant Veracruz Clams

Stir-Fry Vegetables

¼ cup **GRANDMA'S Molasses**
¼ cup **chicken broth**
4 teaspoons **cornstarch**
2 tablespoons **soy sauce**
1 teaspoon **minced garlic**
1 tablespoon **minced ginger**
⅛ teaspoon **ground red pepper**
1 tablespoon **canola oil**
2 pounds **fresh vegetable sliced, bite size (celery, zucchini, onion, peppers, Chinese cabbage and snow peas)**

In large bowl, combine molasses, broth, cornstarch, soy sauce, garlic, ginger and red pepper. Set aside. Heat oil in wok or large heavy skillet. Add vegetables and stir-fry 2 minutes until crisp and tender. Mix in molasses mixture. Cook just until sauce thickens and vegetables are well coated.   *Makes 4 to 6 servings*

Stir-Fry Vegetables

Fillet of Sole

2 tablespoons olive oil
1 medium onion, chopped
1 medium green pepper, chopped
1 ¼ cups **CLAMATO** Tomato Cocktail
½ cup **HOLLAND HOUSE** White Cooking Wine
4 sole fillets (6 ounces each)
  Dash pepper
1 tablespoon lemon juice
2 tablespoons butter
  Lemon slices, for garnish
  Chopped parsley, for garnish

1. Heat oven to 350°F. Heat oil in a sauté pan. Add onion and green pepper; sauté over medium heat about 5 minutes. Stir in Clamato and cooking wine. Lower heat and simmer for 20 to 30 minutes, until sauce is reduced to 1 ¼ cups.

2. Cut each piece of sole in half lengthwise. Roll each fillet and secure with toothpick. Grease 8-inch baking dish, place rolls flat on side so spiral is visible. Sprinkle with pepper; drizzle with lemon juice. Dot with butter. Bake for 15 to 20 minutes. Transfer fillets to serving platter. Stir juice from pan into Clamato mixture. Spoon sauce over fish and garnish with lemon slices and parsley. *Makes 4 servings*

Chicken Primavera

1/4 cup butter
1 pound boneless skinless chicken breasts, cut into strips
8 ounces (about 18 spears) fresh asparagus, cut into 1-inch pieces
2 leeks, rinsed, trimmed and cut into 1/2-inch slices (white part only)
1 cup sliced mushrooms
1 red bell pepper, cut into strips
4 tablespoons HOLLAND HOUSE Vermouth Cooking Wine, divided
1/2 cup whipping cream
1 tablespoon Dijon mustard
1/4 cup grated Parmesan cheese
1/4 teaspoon freshly ground black pepper
1 pound fettuccine, cooked, drained

Melt butter in large pan over medium heat. Add chicken. Cook until chicken is cooked through, about 10 to 12 minutes. Remove from skillet; keep warm. Add asparagus, leeks, mushrooms, red pepper and 2 tablespoons cooking wine to skillet; cook 2 minutes. Remove from skillet; keep warm. Add whipping cream, remaining 2 tablespoons cooking wine and mustard to skillet. Cook until thickened and bubbly, stirring constantly. Add cheese, black pepper, reserved chicken and vegetables; stir to combine. Serve over cooked fettuccine.

Makes 6 servings

Double Cheese Veal Cutlets

    2 tablespoons butter
    1 pound veal cutlets
     Salt and black pepper
    4 cups CLAMATO Tomato Cocktail
     Pinch of thyme
    2 tablespoons Parmesan cheese, grated
    4 ounces Swiss cheese, grated
    1 avocado, peeled and sliced

1. In large skillet, melt butter. Brown cutlets a few at a time, 2 minutes on each side. Remove and sprinkle lightly with salt and pepper.

2. Return veal to skillet, overlapping cutlets. Add Clamato and thyme; simmer 5 to 10 minutes, or until veal is tender. Arrange veal in ovenproof serving dish and pour basting sauce over veal. Sprinkle with Parmesan and Swiss cheese. Place under hot broiler 5 minutes, or until cheese is melted. Top cutlets with avocado slices.   *Makes 6 to 8 servings*

Curried Chicken

    1/4 cup GRANDMA'S Molasses
    1/4 cup lemon juice
    1/4 cup orange juice
    1/4 cup oil
     1 teaspoon curry powder
     6 chicken breasts

Mix molasses, lemon juice, orange juice, oil and curry powder until well blended. Place chicken breasts, skin side down, on broiler rack. Baste chicken breasts with molasses mixture. Broil 10 minutes, basting twice. Turn, baste again and broil 10 minutes more basting 1 more time.*   *Makes 6 servings*

Do not baste during last 5 minutes of cooking.

Double Cheese Veal Cutlets

Mandarin Orange Chicken

⅓ cup **HOLLAND HOUSE** White Cooking Wine
3 ounces frozen orange juice concentrate, thawed
¼ cup orange marmalade
½ teaspoon ground ginger
4 boneless chicken breast halves (about 1 pound)
1 can (11 ounces) mandarin orange segments,
   drained
½ cup green grapes, halved

Heat oven to 350°F. In 12×8-inch (2-quart) baking dish, combine cooking wine, concentrate, marmalade and ginger; mix well. Add chicken; turn to coat. Bake 45 to 60 minutes, or until chicken is tender and no longer pink in center, basting occasionally.* Add orange segments and grapes during last 5 minutes of cooking.

Makes 4 servings

*Do not baste during last 5 minutes of cooking.

Honey Streusel Cake

1½ cups bran flakes
1 cup **MOTT'S Apple Sauce**
4 eggs, slightly beaten
½ cup honey
½ cup butter, melted
⅓ cup skim milk
1½ cups all-purpose flour
¾ cup sugar
2 teaspoons baking powder
Streusel Topping (recipe follows)
Confectioners' sugar (optional)

1. Heat oven to 375°F. In large bowl, mix bran flakes, apple sauce, eggs, honey, butter and milk; let stand 5 minutes. In separate bowl, blend flour, sugar and baking powder; stir in bran mixture just until blended. (Batter will be slightly lumpy.)

2. Spoon batter into greased 9-inch springform pan. Bake 20 minutes. Prepare Streusel Topping. Sprinkle Streusel Topping on top of cake. Return cake to oven and bake 25 minutes more or until toothpick inserted into center comes out clean. Cool in pan on wire rack 20 minutes. Remove from pan; cool completely on wire rack. Dust with confectioners' sugar, if desired.

Makes 12 servings

STREUSEL TOPPING: With mixer, beat ¼ cup butter and ¼ cup sugar until creamy. Stir in 1 cup bran flakes, ¼ cup all-purpose flour and 1 teaspoon ground cinnamon.

BACKYARD BASHES

Barbecued Ribs

1 cup ketchup
½ cup **GRANDMA'S** Molasses
¼ cup cider vinegar
¼ cup Dijon mustard
2 tablespoons Worcestershire sauce
1 teaspoon garlic powder
1 teaspoon hickory flavor liquid smoke (optional)
¼ teaspoon ground red pepper
¼ teaspoon hot pepper sauce
4 to 6 pounds baby back ribs

1. Prepare grill for direct cooking. While coals are heating, combine all ingredients except ribs in large bowl; mix well. Place ribs on grid over medium hot coals. Cook ribs 40 to 45 minutes or until they begin to brown; turning occasionally.

2. Once ribs begin to brown, begin basting them with sauce. Continue to cook and baste ribs with sauce an additional 1 to 1½ hours or until tender and cooked through.*

Makes 4 to 6 servings

Do not baste during last 5 minutes of grilling.

Grilled Sherry Pork Chops

¼ cup **HOLLAND HOUSE Sherry Cooking Wine**
¼ cup **GRANDMA'S Molasses**
2 tablespoons **soy sauce**
4 **pork chops (1-inch) thick**

In plastic bowl, combine sherry, molasses and soy sauce; pour over pork chops. Cover; refrigerate 30 minutes. Prepare grill. Drain pork chops; save marinade. Grill pork chops over medium-high heat 20 to 30 minutes or until pork is no longer pink in center, turning once and brushing frequently with marinade. Discard any remaining marinade.*

Makes 4 servings

Do not baste during last 5 minutes of grilling.

Maui Magic Marinade

1½ cups **MAUNA LA'I Island Guava Juice Drink**
½ cup **pineapple juice**
¼ cup **brown sugar**
2 **large garlic cloves, finely chopped**
½ teaspoon **ginger**
¼ teaspoon **white pepper**
½ cup **oil**

Combine Mauna La'i Island Guava Juice Drink, pineapple juice, brown sugar, garlic, ginger, pepper and oil in plastic bowl. Use with your favoirite chicken, meat or fish recipes.

Makes 2½ cups

Grilled Sherry Pork Chop

Passionate Sorbet

2 cups MAUNA LA'I Paradise Passion Juice Drink
¼ cup sugar
½ envelope of unflavored gelatin

1. Combine Mauna La'i Paradise Passion Juice Drink and sugar in medium sauce pan. Sprinkle gelatin over juice drink and let sit 1 to 2 minutes to soften. Cook on low heat until gelatin and sugar dissolve, stirring occasionally. Pour into 9×9-inch pan and freeze until just firm.

2. Remove from freezer and cut into small pieces. Place frozen pieces in food processor. Process until light and creamy. Return to pan. Cover and freeze until firm. To serve, scrape off thin layers with spoon. *Makes 6 servings*

Crabby Bob's Secret Drink

½ cup MAUNA LA'I Paradise Passion Juice Drink
½ cup MAUNA LA'I ¡Mango Mango! Juice Drink
⅛ cup lemon-lime flavored rum
Splash peach brandy
Lime wedge, as needed
Ice, as needed

Combine Mauna La'i Paradise Passion Juice Drink, Mauna La'i ¡Mango Mango! Juice Drink, rum, and peach brandy in shaker with ice. Pour into glass filled with ice. Garnish with lime wedge. *Makes 1 drink*

Passionate Sorbet

Grilled Fish Florentine

MARINADE:
- ¼ cup oil
- 2 tablespoons lemon juice
- 2 tablespoons soy sauce
- 1 teaspoon grated lemon peel
- 1 garlic clove, minced
- 4 fresh or frozen red snapper or swordfish steaks, thawed

FLORENTINE SAUCE:
- 1 tablespoon butter
- ½ cup chopped scallions
- ¼ cup chopped fresh mushrooms
- 1 cup chicken broth
- ⅓ cup **HOLLAND HOUSE** White Cooking Wine
- ½ cup whipping cream
- 4 cups chopped fresh spinach
- ¼ teaspoon pepper

1. In large plastic bowl, combine oil, lemon juice, soy sauce, lemon peel and garlic; mix well. Add fish, turning to coat all sides. Cover; refrigerate 2 hours. Prepare barbecue grill. Meanwhile, melt butter in large skillet over medium heat. Add scallons and mushrooms; cook until softened, about 3 minutes, stirring occasionally. Stir in chicken broth and cooking wine. Bring to a boil; boil until sauce is reduced by half, about 10 minutes. Add whipping cream; simmer over medium heat until sauce is reduced to about ½ cup, about 10 minutes. Strain into food processor bowl. Add spinach; process until smooth. Add pepper, keep warm.

2. Drain fish, reserving lemon-soy sauce mixture. Place fish on grill over medium-hot coals. Cook 10 minutes or until fish flakes easily with a fork, turning once and brushing frequently with lemon-soy sauce.* Discard any leftover marinade. Serve fish with spinach sauce. *Makes 4 servings*

*Do not marinate during last 5 minutes of cooking.

Grilled Fish Florentine

Sweet 'n Zesty Barbecue Sauce

¾ cup **HOLLAND HOUSE** White Cooking Wine
½ cup **GRANDMA'S** Molasses
½ cup **chili sauce**
¼ cup **prepared mustard**
  1 **small onion, chopped**
  1 **tablespoon Worcestershire sauce**

In medium saucepan, combine all ingredients; mix well. Bring to a boil, reduce heat. Simmer uncovered 10 minutes.

Makes 2 cups

Raspberry Sherbet Punch

1 to 2 liters **HAWAIIAN PUNCH** Fruit Juicy Red
4 cups **club soda**
4 cups **ginger ale**
2 cups **water**
4 cups **raspberry sherbet, divided**

Stir Hawaiian Punch, club soda, ginger ale, water and 2 cups sherbet in large punch bowl. Float remaining 2 cups sherbet in small scoops.

Makes 24 (6-ounce) servings

Tropical Strawberry Freeze

½ cup **MAUNA LA'I Paradise Passion Juice Drink**
¼ cup **frozen strawberries, thawed**
1½ tablespoons **ROSE'S Grenadine**
1 cup **crushed ice**
Strawberry, as needed

Blend Mauna La'i Paradise Passion Juice Drink, strawberries, grenadine and ice in blender on high speed or until thoroughly combined. Pour into glass. Garnish with strawberry.

Makes 1 drink

Mango Margarita

½ cup **MAUNA LA'I ¡Mango Mango! Juice Drink**
1 ounce **tequila**
Dash ROSE'S Triple Sec
Dash ROSE'S Lime Juice
Lime wedge, as needed
Ice, as needed

Combine Mauna La'i ¡Mango Mango! Juice Drink, tequila, triple sec and lime juice in shaker with ice. Pour into salt-rimmed margarita glass. Garnish with lime.

Makes 1 drink

Daiquiri

¾ cup **MAUNA LA'I ¡Mango Mango! Juice Drink**
3 tablespoons rum
1 tablespoon **ROSE'S Lime Juice**
1 teaspoon sugar
Ice, as needed

Combine Mauna La'i ¡Mango Mango! Juice Drink, rum, lime juice and sugar in shaker with ice. Pour into tall glass filled with ice.

Makes 1 drink

Kiwi Margarita

3½ ounces **MR & MRS T Margarita Mix**
2 ripe kiwi, peeled
1 cup strawberry sorbet
1½ ounces white rum
2 ounces club soda
MR & MRS T Margarita Salt (optional)

Blend first 5 ingredients in blender on low speed until smooth.*
Coat rim of glass with lime and dip in margarita salt, if desired.
Pour into glass.

Makes 1 serving

Be careful not to blend too long, crushed kiwi seeds taste bitter.

Clockwise from top: Mango Margarita (page 71), Kiwi Margarita and Daiquiri

Grilled Lemon Chicken Dijon

⅓ cup **HOLLAND HOUSE White with Lemon
   Cooking Wine**
⅓ cup **olive oil**
2 tablespoons **Dijon mustard**
1 teaspoon **dried thyme leaves**
2 **boneless skinless chicken breasts, halved**

1. In shallow baking dish combine cooking wine, oil, mustard and thyme. Add chicken and turn to coat. Cover; marinate in refrigerator for 1 to 2 hours.

2. Prepare grill for direct cooking. Drain chicken, reserving marinade. Grill chicken over medium coals 15 to 20 minutes or until cooked through, turning once and basting with marinade.*

Makes 4 servings

*Do not baste during last 5 minutes of grilling.

Texas Barbecued Ribs

1 cup **GRANDMA'S Molasses**
½ cup **coarse-grained mustard**
2 tablespoons **cider vinegar**
2 teaspoons **dry mustard**
3½ pounds **pork loin baby back ribs or spareribs, cut
   into 6 sections**

Prepare grill for direct cooking. In medium bowl, combine molasses, mustard, cider vinegar and dry mustard. When ready to barbecue, place ribs on grill meaty side up over medium-hot coals. Cook 1 to 1¼ hours or until meat is tender and starts to pull away from bone, basting frequently with sauce* during last 15 minutes of cooking. To serve, cut ribs apart carefully with knife and arrange on platter.   *Makes 4 servings*

*Do not baste during last 5 minutes of grilling.

Grilled Lemon Chicken Dijon

HOLIDAY
MAGIC

GRANDMA'S Gingerbread

½ cup shortening or butter
½ cup sugar
1 cup **GRANDMA'S** Molasses
2 eggs
2½ cups all-purpose flour
1 teaspoon salt
2 teaspoons baking powder
½ teaspoons baking soda
1 teaspoon ginger
2 teaspoons cinnamon
½ teaspoon ground cloves
1 cup hot water

Heat oven to 350°F. In medium bowl, blend shortening with sugar, add molasses and eggs. Beat well. Sift dry ingredients, add alternately with water to molasses mixture. Bake in greased 9-inch square pan, about 50 minutes. *Makes 8 servings*

Barbecued Swedish Meatballs

MEATBALLS
1½ pounds lean ground beef
1 cup finely chopped onions
½ cup fresh breadcrumbs
½ cup **HOLLAND HOUSE** White Cooking Wine
1 egg, beaten
½ teaspoon allspice
½ teaspoon nutmeg

SAUCE
1 jar (10 ounces) currant jelly
½ cup chili sauce
¼ cup **HOLLAND HOUSE** White Cooking Wine
1 tablespoon cornstarch

Heat oven to 350°F. In medium bowl, combine all meatball ingredients, mix well. Shape into 1-inch balls. Place meatballs in 15×10×1-inch baking pan. Bake 20 minutes or until brown.

In medium saucepan, combine all sauce ingredients; mix well. Cook over medium heat until mixture boils and thickens, stirring occasionally. Add meatballs. To serve, place meatballs and sauce in fondue pot or chafing dish. Serve with cocktail picks.

Makes 6 to 8 servings

Barbecued Swedish Meatballs

Apple Sauce Gingerbread Cookies

    4 cups all-purpose flour
    2 teaspoons ground ginger
    2 teaspoons ground cinnamon
    1 teaspoon baking soda
    ½ teaspoon salt
    ¼ teaspoon ground nutmeg
    ½ cup butter, softened
    1 cup sugar
    ⅓ cup GRANDMA'S Molasses
    1 cup MOTT'S Natural Apple Sauce
      Decorator Icing (recipe follows)

1. Heat oven to 350°F. In large bowl, sift together flour, ginger, cinnamon, baking soda, salt and nutmeg; set aside. In bowl of electric mixer, fitted with paddle, beat butter, sugar and molasses until creamy. Alternately blend in dry ingredients and apple sauce. Cover and chill dough for several hours or overnight.

2. On floured surface, roll dough out to ⅛ inch thickness with lightly floured rolling pin. Cut with floured cookie cutter. Place on greased baking sheet. Bake 12 minutes or until done. Remove from sheet; cool on wire rack. Frost with Decorator Icing as desired. After icing dries, store in airtight container.

Makes 2½ dozen (5½-inch tall) cookies

DECORATOR ICING: Mix 2 cups confectioners' sugar and 1 tablespoon water. Add more water, 1 teaspoon at a time, until icing holds its shape and can be piped through decorating tube.

Oatmeal Cookies

1 cup all-purpose flour
1 teaspoon baking powder
½ teaspoon baking soda
½ teaspoon salt
2 tablespoons vegetable shortening
¼ cup **MOTT'S Cinnamon Apple Sauce**
½ cup granulated sugar
½ cup light brown sugar
1 egg *or* ¼ cup egg substitute
1 teaspoon vanilla extract
1⅓ cup rolled oats
½ cup raisins

Heat oven to 375°F. Lightly spray cookie sheet with cooking spray. In large bowl, mix flour, baking powder, baking soda and salt. In separate bowl, whisk together shortening, apple sauce, granulated and brown sugars, egg, and vanilla until shortening breaks into pea sized pieces. Add flour mixture to apple sauce mixture. Mix well. Fold in oats and raisins. Drop rounded teaspoonfuls onto cookie sheet; bake 5 minutes. Remove cookies from cookie sheet and cool completely on wire rack.

Makes 36 cookies

Merry Mango Fizz

1 bottle (64 ounces) MAUNA LA'I ¡Mango Mango! Juice Drink
1 bottle (32 ounces) cranberry juice cocktail
1 bottle (32 ounces) ginger ale
2 cups vanilla ice cream
Fresh or frozen strawberries, as needed

Combine Mauna La'i ¡Mango Mango! Juice Drink, cranberry juice cocktail in a large punch bowl. Fifteen minutes before serving, add ginger ale and ice cream. Do not stir. Garnish with strawberries. *Makes 24 servings*

Mocha Colada

3 ounces MR & MRS T Piña Colada Mix
1 ounce COCO CASA Cream of Coconut
2 ounces cold espresso (or other strong coffee)
1 cup ice
½ tablespoon chocolate syrup
Chocolate covered espresso bean, for garnish

Blend first 4 ingredients in blender until slushy. Pour into tall glass and garnish with chocolate syrup and espresso bean.
Makes 1 serving

Left to right: Merry Mango Fizz, Mocha Colada and Toasted Coco Colada (page 84)

Toasted Coco Colada

      3 ounces MR & MRS T Piña Colada Mix
1 ½ ounces coconut rum
   ½ ounce caramel syrup
   ½ ounce coconut syrup
    1 cup ice
    1 lime wedge
      Toasted coconut flakes, ground (as needed)

Blend first 5 ingredients in blender until slushy. Coat rim of
daiquiri glass with lime wedge, dip glass into ground toasted
coconut flakes. Pour into daiquiri glass.   *Makes 1 drink*

Quick Hot Spiced Cider

    8 cups MOTT'S Apple Juice
    2 tablespoons brown sugar
    1 teaspoon whole allspice
    1 teaspoon whole cloves
    8 cinnamon sticks

Combine apple juice, brown sugar, allspice and cloves in large
pot. Bring to boil, then simmer 15 minutes. Remove cloves and
allspice. Add cinnamon stick to each mug before serving.
                                              Makes 8 servings

Harvest Bundt Cake

2½ cups all-purpose flour
1 tablespoon baking powder
2 teaspoons ground cinnamon
1½ teaspoons baking soda
½ teaspoon ground nutmeg
1½ cups boiling water
1½ cups bran flakes
1 cup firmly packed light brown sugar
1 cup seedless raisins
½ cup butter
1 cup MOTT'S Apple Sauce
2 eggs, beaten

Heat oven to 350°F. In large bowl, mix flour, baking powder, cinnamon, baking soda and nutmeg; set aside. In separate bowl, combine water, bran flakes, brown sugar, raisins and butter; let stand 5 minutes. Stir in apple sauce, eggs and flour mixture. Spoon into greased and floured 12-cup fluted tube pan. Bake 50 minutes or until toothpick inserted into cake comes out clean. Cool in pan on wire rack 20 minutes. Remove cake from pan and cool completely on wire rack.

Makes 12 to 16 servings

Pumpkin Bread

 1 package (about 18 ounces) yellow cake mix
 1 can (16 ounces) solid pack pumpkin
 ⅓ cup **GRANDMA'S Molasses**
 4 eggs
 1 teaspoon cinnamon
 1 teaspoon nutmeg
 ⅓ cup nuts, chopped (optional)
 ⅓ cup raisins (optional)

1. Heat oven to 350°F. Grease two 9×5-inch loaf pans.

2. Combine all ingredients in large bowl and mix well. Beat at medium speed 2 minutes. Pour into prepared pans. Bake 60 minutes or until toothpick inserted in center comes out clean. *Makes 2 loaves*

TIP: *Serve with cream cheese or preserves, or top with cream cheese frosting or ice cream.*

Pumpkin Bread

Brownie Apple Sauce Cake

½ cup butter
3 squares (I ounce each) unsweetened chocolate
I cup sugar
1½ cups MOTT'S Apple Sauce
3 eggs, well beaten
I teaspoon vanilla extract
1½ cups all-purpose flour
I teaspoon baking soda
½ teaspoon salt
½ cup chopped walnuts
Apple Cream Cheese Frosting (recipe follows)

I. Heat oven to 350°F. In large heavy saucepan, over low heat, melt butter and chocolate, stirring constantly. Remove from heat and cool. Blend sugar, apple sauce, eggs and vanilla into chocolate mixture. In large bowl, mix flour, baking soda and salt. With wooden spoon, stir in chocolate mixture until blended. Stir in walnuts.

2. Pour batter into 2 greased and floured 8-inch round cake pans. Bake 35 to 40 minutes or until toothpick inserted in center comes out clean. Cool in pans 10 minutes. Prepare Apple Cream Cheese Frosting. Remove from pans; cool completely on wire racks. Fill and frost with Apple Cream Cheese Frosting.

Makes 12 servings

APPLE CREAM CHEESE FROSTING: In large bowl, beat 2 packages (8 ounces each) softened cream cheese and ½ cup softened butter until light and fluffly. Blend in 1 cup confectioners' sugar, ½ cup MOTT'S Apple Sauce, ½ cup melted and cooled caramels and 1 teaspoon vanilla extract.

Brownie Apple Sauce Cake

Golden Apple Cupcakes

    1 package (18 to 20 ounces) yellow cake mix
    1 cup MOTT'S Chunky Apple Sauce
    ⅓ cup vegetable oil
    3 eggs
    ¼ cup firmly packed light brown sugar
    ¼ cup chopped walnuts
    ½ teaspoon ground cinnamon
      Vanilla Frosting (recipe follows)

Heat oven to 350°F. In bowl, combine cake mix, apple sauce, oil and eggs; blend according to package directions. Spoon batter into 24 paper-lined muffin pan cups. Mix brown sugar, walnuts and cinnamon; sprinkle over prepared batter in muffin cups. Bake 20 to 25 minutes or until toothpick inserted in center comes out clean. Cool in pan 10 minutes. Remove from pan; cool completely on wire rack. Frost cupcakes with Vanilla Frosting.

Makes 24 cupcakes

VANILLA FROSTING: In large bowl, beat 1 package (8 ounces) softened cream cheese until light and creamy; blend in ¼ teaspoon vanilla extract. Beat ½ cup heavy cream until stiff; fold into cream cheese mixture.

Spiced Gingerbread

1½ cups bran flakes
1 cup milk
1½ cups all-purpose flour
2 teaspoons baking soda
1 teaspoon ground cinnamon
1 teaspoon ground ginger
½ teaspoon ground cloves
1 cup **GRANDMA'S Molasses**
½ cup butter, melted
3 eggs
Confectioners' sugar (optional)

1. Heat oven to 350°F. In large bowl, mix bran flakes and milk; let stand 5 minutes. In separate bowl, mix flour, baking soda, cinnamon, ginger and cloves; set aside. In another bowl, with electric mixer at medium speed, beat molasses, butter and eggs until smooth. Blend in bran and flour mixtures. Pour batter into greased and floured 13×9×2-inch baking pan.

2. Bake 40 to 45 minutes or until toothpick inserted in center comes out clean. Cool in pan 10 minutes. Remove from pan; cool completely on wire rack. Sprinkle with confectioners' sugar if desired; cut into 2½×2 inch pieces to serve.

Makes 20 servings

Festive Holiday Punch

- 8 cups MOTT'S Apple Juice
- 8 cups cranberry juice cocktail
- 2 red apples, sliced
- 2 cups cranberries
- 3 liters lemon-lime soda
  Ice cubes, as needed

Pour apple and cranberry juices into punch bowl. Fifteen minutes before serving, add apple slices, cranberries, soda and ice. Do not stir. *Makes 24 servings*

Apple Sauce with Crunchy Topping

- ¾ cup bran flakes
- ¼ cup finely chopped pecans
- 3 tablespoons firmly packed light brown sugar
- 2 tablespoons butter
- 1½ cups MOTT'S Apple Sauce, any variety

In medium bowl, mix bran flakes and pecans; set aside. In saucepan, over medium heat, heat brown sugar and butter until melted and blended. Remove from heat; add bran mixture, tossing to coat well. Cool. Spoon apple sauce into 6 (6-ounce) dessert dishes; top with bran mixture. Serve immediately.

Makes 6 servings

Festive Holiday Punch

Holiday Wassail

I gallon MOTT'S Apple Juice
I quart orange juice
I can (16 ounces) frozen pineapple juice, thawed
2 cups lemon juice
2 cinnamon sticks
2 teaspoons cloves
I cup sugar

Place all ingredients in non-aluminum pan, stir, and heat to
boiling. Simmer for one hour. Serve hot.   *Makes 24 servings*

Apple Snow

I ½ cups MOTT'S Apple Juice
I tablespoon honey
3 cups ice

Place apple juice, honey and ice in blender and blend until finely
crushed or to consistency of snow. Serve immediately.
Makes 2 servings

Index